Happines

DEMAND TO BE GRATIFIED

Happiness Comes To Those
Who Ask And Search For It

BESSIE ORTEGA

Table of Contents

Chapter 1:

The People You Need in Your Life

We all have friends, the people that are there for us and would be there no matter what. These people don't necessarily need to be different, and these traits might all be in one person. Friends are valuable. You only really ever come across ones that are real. In modern-day society, it's so hard to find friends that want to be your friends rather than just to use you.

Sometimes the few the better, but you need some friends that would guide you along your path. We all need them, and you quite possibly have these traits too. Your friends need you, and you may not even know it.

1. The Mentor

No matter which area or field they are trying to excel in, the common denominator is that they have clarity about life and know exactly what their goals are. These people can impact you tremendously, helps you get into the winners' mindset, infuse self-belief and confidence in you then you, too, can succeed and accomplish your goals. They act as a stepping stone for you to get through your problems. They are happy for your success and would guide you through the troubles and problems while trying to get there.

2. Authentic People

You never feel like you have to make pretense around these people. Life can be challenging enough, so having friends that aren't judging you and are being themselves is very important for your well-being. This type of friend allows you to be vulnerable, express your emotion in healthy ways, and helps bring a smile back to your face when you're down.

They help you also show your true self and how you feel. Rather than showing only a particular side of their personality, they open their whole self to you, allowing you to do the same and feel comfortable around them.

3. Optimists

These people are the kind you need, the ones that will encourage you through tough times. They will be there encouraging you, always seeing the best in the situation. Having the ability to see the best in people and will always have an open mind to situations. Everyone needs optimism in their lives, and these people bring that.

"Optimism is essential to achievement, and it is also the foundation of courage and true progress." -Nicholas M. Butler.

4. Brutally Honest People

To have a balanced view of yourself and be aware of your blind spots is important for you. Be around people who would provide authentic feedback and not sugarcoat while giving an honest opinion about you. They will help you be a better version of yourself, rectifying your mistakes, work on your weak spots, and help you grow. These are the people you can hang around to get better, and you will critique yourself but in a good way, helping you find the best version of yourself. Of course, the ones that are just rude should be avoided, and they should still be nice to you but not too nice to the point where they compliment you even when they shouldn't.

Chapter 2:

Happy People View Problems as Challenges

To state the obvious: It's easier to be happy when things are going well. Positive outcomes are known to lift people's moods, while negative emotions (like anxiety) generally reflect concerns about negative outcomes.

But, happy people are also good at dealing with problems in ways that help them to maintain their mood, while still dealing with issues effectively. Here are three common things that happy people tend to do to deal with speed bumps in life.

FOCUS ON THE FUTURE

It is important to understand the problem you're facing, and so happy people certainly analyze the situation. But, they don't remain focused on the problem for long. That is, they avoid rumination—which is a set of repeated thoughts about something that has gone wrong.

Instead, they look to the future. There are two benefits to this: One is that the future is not determined yet, and so happy people can be optimistic about things to come. The other is that happy people are looking to make the future better than the past, which creates a hopeful outlook—no matter what the present circumstances look like.

FIND AGENCY

At any given moment, the situation you are in exerts some amount of control over your options. When you're sitting in traffic, for example, there isn't much you can do but wait for the cars around you to start moving. The amount of control you have to take action in a situation is your degree of agency.

Happy people seek out their sources of agency when problems arise. They are most interested in what they can do to influence the situation, rather than focusing on all of the options that have been closed off by what has happened. The focus on agency is important, because it provides the basis for creating a plan to solve the problem. And the sooner a problem is addressed, the less time it has to cause stress.

KNOW WHEN TO FOLD

There are always going to be big problems that you can't solve. Perhaps there is a client who is never satisfied with the work you do. Maybe there is a process you're trying to implement that never seems to have the desired outcome. You might even have been working on the problem for a long time.

Despite all the discussions about the importance of grit, effective (and happy) problem solvers are good at knowing when to walk away from a problem that can't be fixed. Each of us has a limited amount of time and energy that we can devote to the work we are doing. Spending time on problems that cannot be solved has an opportunity cost. There are other things you could be doing with your time that might yield better outcomes. It is important to learn when it is time to give up on a problem rather than continuing to try to solve it.

This is particularly true when you have been working on that problem for a long time. There is a tendency for people to pay attention to sunk costs—the time, money, and energy they have already devoted to working on something. But, those resources are gone, and you can't get them back. If it isn't likely that additional effort is going to help you solve a problem, then you should walk away, no matter how hard you have worked on it already. Happy people are good at ignoring those sunk costs both when making the decision to walk away from a project and after making the decision to walk away. They don't spend time regretting the "wasted" resources.

Chapter 3:

Happy People Surround Themselves with The Right People

Whether we realized it or not, we become like the five people we spend the most time with. We start behaving like them, thinking like them, looking like them. We even make decisions based on what we think they would want us to do.

For example, there are many research findings that prove we are more likely to gain weight if a close friend or a family member becomes overweight. Similarly, we are more likely to engage in an exercise program if we surround ourselves with fit and health-oriented people.

So, who are the top 5 influencers in your life? Do they make you feel positive? Do they inspire and motivate you to be the best version of yourself? Do they support and encourage you to achieve your goals? Or, do they tell you that "it can't be done," "it's not possible," "you aren't good enough," "you will most likely fail."

If you feel emotionally drained by the energetic vampires in your life, you may want to detox your life and get rid of the relationships that aren't serving you in a positive way.

The negative people, the naysayers, the Debbie Downers, and the chronic complainers are like a dark cloud over your limitless potential.

They hold you back and discourage you from even trying because they're afraid that if you succeed, you'll prove them wrong.

Have the courage to remove the negative people from your life and watch how your energy and enthusiasm automatically blossom. Letting go of the relationships that aren't serving us is a critical step if we want to become more positive, fulfilled, and successful.

Detoxing your life from negative influencers will also allow you to become the person you truly want to be. You'll free yourself from constant judgment, negativity, and lack of support.

Here's what you can do:

- Stay away from chronic complainers.
- Stop participating in meaningless conversations.
- Share your ideas only with people who are supportive or willing to provide constructive criticism.
- Minimize your interactions with "friends," coworkers, and family members who are negative, discouraging, and bitter.
- Stop watching TV and reading negative posts on social media (yes, mainstream media is a major negative influence in our lives!).
- Surround yourself with positive and successful people (remember, we become like the top 5 people we spend our time with!).

- Find new, like-minded friends, join networking and support groups, or find a positive coach or a mentor.

If you want to make a positive change in your life, remember, the people around you have a critical influence on your energy, growth, and probability of success.

Positive people bring out the best in you and make you feel motivated and happy. They help you when you're in need, encourage you to go after your dreams, and are there to celebrate your successes or support you as you move past your challenges. Pick your top 5 wisely!

Chapter 4:

It's Okay To Feel Uncertain

We are surrounded by a world that has endless possibilities. A world where no two incidents can predict the other. A realm where we are a slave to the unpredictable future and its repercussions.

Everyone has things weighing on their mind. Some of us know it and some of us keep carrying these weights unknowingly.

The uncertainty of life is the best gift that you never wanted. But when you come to realize the opportunities that lie at every uneven corner are worth living for.

Life changes fast, sometimes in our favor and sometimes not much. But life always has a way to balance things out. We only need to find the right approach to make things easier for us and the ones around us.

Everyone gets tested once in a while, but we need to find ways to cope with life when things get messy.

The worst thing the uncertainty of life can produce is the fear in your heart. The fear to never know what to expect next. But you can never let fear rule you.

To worry about the future ahead of us is pointless. So change the question from 'What if?' to 'What will I do if.'

If you already have this question popping up in your brain, this means that you are already getting the steam off.

You don't need to fear the uncertain because you can never wreck your life in any such direction from where there is no way back.

The uncertainty of life is always a transformation period to make you realize your true path. These uncertainties make you realize the faults you might have in your approach to things.

You don't need to worry about anything unpredictable and unexpected because not everything is out of your control every time. Things might not happen in a way you anticipated but that doesn't mean you cannot be prepared for it.

There are a lot of things that are in your control and you are well researched and well equipped to go around events. So use your experience to do the damage control.

Let's say you have a pandemic at your hand which you couldn't possibly predict, but that doesn't mean you cannot do anything to work on its effects. You can raise funds for the affected population. You can try to find new ways to minimize unemployment. You can find alternate ways to keep the economy running and so on.

Deal with your emotions as you cannot get carried away with such events being driven by your feelings.

Don't avoid your responsibilities and don't delay anything. You have to fulfill every task expected of you because you were destined to do it. The results are not predetermined on a slate but you can always hope for the best be the best version of yourself no matter how bad things get.

Life provides us with endless possibilities because when nothing is certain, anything is possible. So be your own limit.

Chapter 5:

Doing The Thing You Love Most

Today we are going to talk about following your heart and just going for your passion, even if it ends up being a hobby project.

Many of us have passions that we want to pursue. Whether it be a sport, a fitness goal, a career goal, or simply just doing something we know we are good at. Something that electrifies our soul. Something that really doesn't require much persuasion for us to just go do it on a whim.

Many of us dare not pursue this passion because people have told us time and time again that it will not lead to anywhere. Or maybe it is that voice inside your head that is telling you you should just stick to the practical things in life. Whatever the reasons may be, that itch always seem to pester us, calling out to us, even though we have tried our best to put it aside.

We know what our talents are, and the longer we don't put it out there in the world, the longer we keep it bottled up inside of us, the longer the we will regret it. Personally, Music has always been something that has been calling out to me since i was 15. I've always dabbled in and out of it, but never took it seriously. I found myself 14 years later, wondering how much i could've achieved in the music space if i had just leaned in to it just a little.

I decided that I had just about put it off for long enough and decided to pursue music part time. I just knew deep down inside me that if i did not at least try, that i was going to regret it at some point again in the future.

It is true that passions come and go. We may jump from passion to passion over the course of our lives, and that is okay. But if that thing has been there calling out to you for years or even decades, maybe you should pay closer attention to it just a little more.

Make your passion a project. Make it a hobby. Pursue it in one form or another. We may never be able to make full careers out of our passions, but we can at least incorporate it into our daily lives like a habit. You may find ourselves happier and more fulfilled should you tap that creative space in you that has always been there.

Sure life still takes precedence. Feeding the family, earning that income, taking care of that child. But never for one second think that you should sacrifice doing what truly makes you happy for all of that other stuff, no matter how important. Even as a hobby, pursuing it maybe 30mins a day, or even just an hour a week. It is a start and it is definitely better than nothing.

At the end of the day passions are there to feed our soul. To provide it will some zest and life to our otherwise mundane lives. The next time you hear that voice again, lean in to it. Don't put it off any longer.

Chapter 6:

8 Tips to Become More Resilient

Resilience shows how well you can deal with the problems life throws at you and how you bounce back. It also means whether you maintain a positive outlook and cope with stress effectively or lose your cool. Although some people are naturally resilient, research shows that these behaviors can be learned. So, whether you are going through a tough time right now or you want to be prepared for the next step in your life, here are eight techniques you can focus on to become more resilient.

1. Find a Sense of Purpose

When you are going through a crisis or a tragedy, you must find a sense of purpose for yourself; this can play an important role in your recovery. This can mean getting involved in your community and participating in activities that are meaningful to you so every day you would have something to look forward to, and your mind wouldn't be focusing on the tragedy solely. You will be able to get through the day.

2. Believe in Your Abilities

When you have confidence in yourself that you can cope with the issues in your life, it will play an important role in resilience; once you become confident in your abilities, it will be easier for you to respond and deal with a crisis. Listen to the negative comments in your head, and once you do, you need to practice replacing them with positive comments like I'm good at my job, I can do this, I am a great friend/partner/parent.

3. Develop a Strong Social Network

It is very important to be surrounded by people you can talk to and confide in. When you have caring and supportive people around you during a crisis, they act as your protectors and make that time easier for you. When you are simply talking about your problems with a friend or a family member, it will, of course, not make your problem go away. Still, it allows you to share your feelings and get supportive feedback, and you might even be able to come up with possible solutions to your problems.

4. Embrace Change

An essential part of resilience is flexibility, and you can achieve that by learning how to be more adaptable. You'll be better equipped to respond to a life crisis when you know this. When a person is resilient, they use such events as opportunities to branch out in new directions. However, it is very likely for some individuals to get crushed by abrupt changes, but when it comes to resilient individuals, they adapt to changes and thrive.

5. Be Optimistic

It is difficult to stay optimistic when you are going through a dark period in your life, but an important part of resilience can maintain a hopeful outlook. What you are dealing with can be extremely difficult, but what will help you is maintaining a positive outlook about a brighter future. Now, positive thinking certainly does not mean that you ignore your problem to focus on the positive outcomes. This simply means understanding that setbacks don't always stay there and that you certainly have the skills and abilities to fight the challenges thrown at you.

6. Nurture Yourself

When you are under stress, it is easy not to take care of your needs. You can lose your appetite, ignore exercise, not get enough sleep. These are all very common reactions when you are stressed or are in a situation of crisis. That is why it is important to invest time in yourself, build yourself, and make time for activities you enjoy.

7. Develop Problem-Solving Skills

Research shows that when people are able to come up with solutions to a problem, it is easier for them to cope with problems compared to those who can not. So, whenever you encounter a new challenge, try making a list of potential ways you will be able to solve that problem. You can experiment with different strategies and eventually focus on developing a logical way to work through those problems. By practicing your problem-solving skills on a regular basis, you will be better prepared to cope when a serious challenge emerges.

8. Establish Goals

Crisis situations can be daunting, and they also seem insurmountable but resilient people can view these situations in a realistic way and set reasonable goals to deal with problems. So, when you are overwhelmed by a situation, take a step back and simply assess what is before you and then brainstorm possible solutions to that problem and then break them down into manageable steps.

Chapter 7:

Happy People Live Slow

"Slow Living means **structuring your life around meaning and fulfilment**. Similar to 'voluntary simplicity and 'downshifting,' it emphasizes a **less-is-more approach**, focusing on the quality of your life…Slow Living addresses the desire to lead a more balanced life and pursue a **more holistic sense of well-being** in the fullest sense of the word. In addition to the personal advantages, there are potential **environmental benefits** as well. When we slow down, we often use fewer resources and produce less waste, both of which have a lighter impact on the earth."

Slow living is a state of mind it will make you feel purposeful and is more fulfilling. It is all about being consistent and steady. Now that you have an idea of slow living, we will break down some myths attached to slow living and how to start slow living for mind peace and happiness. The first myth is that slow living is about doing everything as slowly as possible. Slow living is not about doing everything in slow motion but doing things at the right speed and not rushing. It is all about gaining time so you can do things that are important to you. The second myth is that slow living is the same as simple living. Now simple living is more worldly, and simple living is more focused on time.

The third myth is that slow living is an aesthetic that you see on desaturated Instagram posts, but that is not true; this is considered a minimalist aesthetic, whereas slow living is a minimalist lifestyle. The 4th myth is that slow living is about doing and being less. That is not at all true. It is all about removing the non-essentials from your life so you can have more time to be yourself. And the last myth is that slow living is anti-technology now. This is not about travelling back in time but all about using tech as a tool and not vice versa.

If you like this idea of living, we are going to list ten ways in which you can start slow living;

1. Define what is most important to you(essentials)
2. Say no to everything else (non-essentials)
3. Understand busyness and that it is a choice
4. Create space and margin in your day and life
5. Practice being present
6. Commit to putting your life before work
7. Adopt a slow information diet
8. Get outside physically and connect dots mentally
9. Start slow and small by downshifting
10. Find inspiration in the slow living community

Sit back and think about what the purpose of your life is, what you ultimately want from your life and not just in a monetary sense. Think about what you would like for your lifestyle to be 50 years from now, and then start working on it today. Suppose you have not figured out the purpose. In that case, there are multiple personality tests available on the internet that will help you determine your personality type and then eventually help you create your purpose.

Chapter 8:

Make Friends With Your Problems

Today we're going to talk about a topic that I hope will inspire you to view your problems not as a hurdle to your goals, but a necessity. How you can make friends with your problems to eventually see it as a part of your journey towards greater success.

You see, problems arise in all aspects of our lives every single day. As we go through life, we start to realise that life is merely about problem solving. When we are growing up, we face the problems of not being able to stand on our own two feet, problems about not being able to potty train, problems with peeing in the bed, problems with riding a new bicycle, problems with school, problems with Teachers, problems with our homework.

But the thing is that as kids, we view these problems as challenges. As something to work towards. We don't necessarily view problems as a negative thing, and we always strive to overcome these problems, never giving up until we do so. And through this perseverance, we grow and evolve. But as we get older, and our child-like response to problems start to change, we start seeing problems in a different way. Problems become obstacles rather than challenges, and problems sometimes overwhelm us to the point where we are not able to function.

We face problems in getting into good high schools and universities, problems in getting a job, problems with family, problems with relationships, problems with bosses, problems with colleagues, problems with starting a family. All these are legitimate problems that I am very sure every single one of us will face at some point in our lives. And the problems will never stop coming.

From what I have shared so far, it is very clear that problems are a way of life, and problems will never go away. A life without problems is really not life at all.

Personally, I have dealt with my fair share of problems. I struggled greatly with getting good grades in university, I struggled in serving for the army as part of mandatory conscription for my country, I struggled with pressures from work, and these problems at times got to me where I felt that I could not see the light at the end of the tunnel. These problems consumed my vision that I could not see the big picture. That life is beautiful, and that my problems are nothing compared to what life has to offer.

In that moment as I was living through those problems however, I could not see the light. I was laser focused on the problem at hand and at many stages, I did feel depressed. I felt unworthy. I felt like I couldn't handle my problems.

I am not sure if my inability to handle problems as I grew older were genetic, or that my character just wasn't strong enough to withstand pressures from the external world. But I did feel like it became harder and harder each year.

What I failed to realise, and that goes back to how I saw problems when I was young, was that I viewed my problems as an enemy rather than a friend. I saw my problems as something that was getting in the way of my goals, rather than a necessary part of the process towards that goal.

By the time I was 20, I wanted a life without problems. I didn't want to deal with any more problems anymore. And as unrealistic as that sounded, I actually believed that it was what I wanted. And every problem that came my way felt like a mountain. A major annoyance that would take every ounce of my energy to overcome. And that negative view to problems actually made my life much more miserable.

It was only in my late twenties that I saw more of life did my perception of problems start to shift profoundly. I learned of the struggles that my parents had to go through to get the life that I was living today, I saw in many of my peers that work life is actually tough and those that viewed their job negatively almost always ended up depressed and unworthy while those that saw their work as challenges actually grew as people.

That shift happened gradually but I started to see the problems that came up in my daily life as friends rather than as enemies. I started to view the mandatory things I had to do to sustain myself financially, emotionally, physically, as simply a way of life. In areas such as health and fitness where I tend to struggle with a lot, which was quite a big problem in my opinion, i simply found alternative ways to keep fit that worked for me rather than get obsessed with the way i looked.

In areas of finance and career, where I also saw as a big problem, I adapted by adopting a completely novel way of working that actually made my work much more meaningful and enjoyable instead of subscribing myself to a job that I know that I would hate.

I started to view each problem as challenges again that would require my knowledge and expertise to overcome. And it started to consume me less and less. I made them my friends instead of my enemy. And when one door closes, I was always resourceful to find another open door to get me to where I wanted to go.

So I challenge each and everyone of you to start seeing your problems not as hindrances to your goals, but as challenges that requires your smartness to conquer. I believe that you have the power to knock down every problem that comes your way no matter how great the challenge is. However if it does become overwhelming, it is okay to walk away from it. Don't let it consume you and don't obsess over a problem until it wrecks your health mentally and physically. Life is too short for problems to ruin us. If it can't be made friends with, it is okay to simply let it go. Nothing good can come from sheer force.

Chapter 9:

<u>How to Eat With Mood in Mind</u>

At the point when you're feeling down, it tends to be enticing to go to food to lift your spirits. Notwithstanding, the sweet, fatty treats that numerous individuals resort to have unfortunate results of their own. Along these lines, you may puzzle over whether any good food sources can work on your temperament.

As of late, research on the connection between sustenance and psychological wellness has been arising. However, note that state of mind can be impacted by numerous variables, like pressure, climate, helpless rest, hereditary qualities, mood disorders, and nutritional deficiencies. In any case, certain food varieties have been displayed to further develop general mental wellbeing and specific kinds of temperament issues.

1. Fatty Fish

Omega-3 unsaturated fats are a gathering of fundamental fats you should get through your eating routine because your body can't produce them all alone. Fatty fish like salmon and tuna fish are wealthy in two sorts of omega-3s — docosahexaenoic corrosive (DHA) and eicosapentaenoic corrosive (EPA) — that are connected to bring down degrees of despair. Omega-3s add to lower your depression and seem to assume key parts in mental health and cell flagging.

2. Dark Chocolate

Chocolate is wealthy in numerous mood-boosting compounds. Its sugar may further develop mood since it's a fast wellspring of fuel for your brain. Besides, it's anything but a course of feel-great mixtures, like caffeine, theobromine, and N-acylethanolamine — a substance synthetically like cannabinoids that have been connected to improved mood.

3. Fermented Food Varieties

Fermented food sources, which incorporate kimchi, yogurt, kefir, fermented tea, and sauerkraut, may further develop gut wellbeing and state of mind. The fermentation interaction permits live microbes to flourish in food varieties ready to change over sugars into liquor and acids. During this interaction, probiotics are made. These live microorganisms support the development of solid microscopic organisms in your gut and may expand serotonin levels.

4. Bananas

Bananas may assist with flipping around a frown.

They're high in nutrient B6, which orchestrates feel-great synapses like dopamine and serotonin.

Moreover, one enormous banana (136 grams) gives 16 grams of sugar and 3.5 grams of fiber.

When matched with fiber, sugar is delivered gradually into your circulation system, considering stable glucose levels and better disposition control. Glucose levels that are too low may prompt irritability and emotional episodes.

5. Oats

Oats are an entire grain that can keep you feeling great the entire morning. You can appreciate them in numerous structures, like, for the time being, oats, oatmeal, muesli, and granola. They're a phenomenal wellspring of fiber, giving 8 grams in a solitary crude cup (81 grams). Fiber eases back your processing of carbs, considering a slow arrival of sugar into the circulation system to keep your energy levels stable.

Chapter 10:

Just Try

Today we're going to talk about a very simple yet important topic. And my goal for this video to see if i can challenge to get you to try something new every day if you feel that your life isn't exciting or have become somewhat stale.

Have you ever come across the saying " you never know until you try"? This explorative mindset has allowed us as children to experience new things, new food, new activities, make you new friends,and to be curious about everything around us. With this curiosity comes a deeper understanding of our likes and dislikes. And we spend more time on the activity that we really and discard those that we don't favour. Some of these likes can turn into solid passions and even careers that we dedicate our lives to, while some other activities we would soon outgrow and move on from.

Regardless of whether we do stick on to these new interests or not is not of importance. What is however, is that we gave ourselves a chance to have a taste of whether something we have not done before could potentially fit into our lives. We gave it an opportunity to be assimilated into our daily routine and activities. And we find new hobbies left and right that make up our identity. Even in school we are encouraged to try new CCAs, new sports, new musical groups to find something we might like besides studying all day to become a more holistic individual. And even in higher education, universities, we are encouraged to explore different subjects if you are in the field of humanities before you settle down on a major that really speaks to you. And many a times we find that we didn't know we liked something until we really gave it a shot.

However as we grow older, which I'm sure many of you experience as well, our sense of curiosity for the things around us starts to diminish with accelerating pace every year. There is no one around us encouraging us to keep up that level of exploration, and when we are left to our own devices, we stop trying new things. We stop looking for things to learn, stop looking for skills to pick up, and we just settle on the things we have already been doing for so long until it bores us to no end. This lack of exploration can seep into our identity, to the point where we stop trying new food, stop finding new friends, or stop putting ourselves in vulnerable positions where we may feel disappointed if things don't work out. We become so cyclical in the way we view life that fear drives us not to venture outside our comfort zone. This fear holds us back from new experiences and we tend to believe at our age of 25 or whatever, that our identity is fixed and that is who we are until the day we die. We stop exploring new job opportunities that are not within our area of expertise, and we stop trying to step out into the unknown for fear of failure.

But if you realize, the great innovators of the world never ceased to try new things no matter at what age they are at. They do not fear the unknown but yet embrace it. Think Steve Jobs, after being ousted Apple, the company he founded, he made Pixar animations into such a remarkable and industry leading animation studio that he came back to Apple and made it one of the most successful companies of all time. He kept trying to make a difference and he tried new opportunities even after the seemingly huge failure of being kicked out of your own company.

Personally, I never stopped trying new things. I am the kind of person that gets bored very easily after working on something for 1 to 2 years, or maybe a maximum of 3 years. When something becomes too simple that it requires no brain power on your part, the task becomes monotonous and robotic. There were many times i felt that there was no purpose in doing such tasks because I wasn't learning anything new. And when I had that mindset of trying something else that might interest me, suddenly that new thing became exciting and I had something to look forward to learning all over again. Even if it meant that it made little to no money as you tried to make an income stream of it at the beginning stages. I was happy nonetheless.

Think back on the times when you genuinely felt good when you tried something new for the first time and it became something you couldn't possibly move forward without. It could be an apple product, and smartphone tablet or headphones, or a job where your creativity is celebrated, or a new sport or hobby that you have no qualms setting aside countless hours in the week to do. These are all products of simply just trying.

Now look back again and think about when was the last time you actually tried something new. If you can't remember when, it was probably too long ago. You may want to consider making trying new things a habit so much so that it just becomes a part of you.

So i challenge each and everyone of you today to say yes to new experiences, things, and people when the next opportunity comes around. You never know what you may be missing out on. And it could potentially be your next passion in life.

Chapter 11:

<u>How Ditching Your Phone Can Make You Happier</u>

Where is your smartphone at present? Odds are it is close to you, and on the off chance that it vibrates or dings, you will quit perusing this article and verify who messaged you or what occurred on Twitter. Perhaps you remember you're dependent on your smartphone and all that accompanies it, or possibly you don't believe it's something awful to be continually associated with. Regardless, if your smartphone is always with you and always looking at it, you could utilize a break. Unplugging from social media and innovation is frightening for many individuals; however, it doesn't need to be. It could be a truly extraordinary encounter.

Here's why.

Technology has made it simple for individuals to reach others every minute of every day, for better or worse. Your friend can call at 2 a.m. at the point when she needs a ride home, yet your supervisor can likewise call at 10 p.m. at the point when he needs you to assemble into a conference — presently. You can reconnect with old friends from secondary school, yet your greatest enemy is continually posting her most recent achievements, causing you to feel less and inadequate.

The surge of texts, notifications, emails, and calls implies your mind is consistently on high alarm, sitting tight for the next ding. You can never genuinely unwind, except if your telephone is off. Believe it or not. Not on vibrate, off. By turning your phone off for even 20 minutes, you can give your cerebrum, body, and feelings a break from the consistent commitment. You can zero in on the book you're perusing, give your cherished ones your full focus, completely appreciate the film you're watching and shut your brain off when you're attempting to rest.

Numerous individuals have had a go at unplugging, regardless of whether it be for five minutes or a whole year. While a few groups say from the outset, they felt restless and disrupted, they, at last, started to see the value in the time to themselves. There's no commitment to answer your cell phone when you don't hear it ring, no strain to "like" your dearest companion's latest status when you didn't see it. Moving back from these "responsibilities" allows you an opportunity to truly be with yourself or with your loved ones. With your cellphone on, a piece of you is consistent with individuals posting on Snapchat and messaging you. With no time really for yourself, you can begin to feel excessively pushed or discouraged.

Chapter 12:

Happy People Consciously Nurture A Growth Mindset

"Without continual growth and progress, such words as improvement, achievement, and success have no meaning." – Benjamin Franklin

Learning is perceived and generally acknowledged by those of us who have gone through primary and university tutoring. We were routinely encircled by people who energized and upheld our developments. Ground-breaking thoughts and change were anticipated from us; the sky was the limit!! However, shouldn't something be said about once we got into the work environment? For some, we subsided into the everyday daily practice, getting it done, uninformed of the cost that our agreeable, monotonous, continuous tasks appeared to have on our own and expert development.

Do you hear employees saying, "I don't get how this venture's development works" or "I'm awful at giving introductions. If it's not too much trouble, let another person do it." If this is the case, reconsideration of your group's growth mindset might be in order. They are working under a "fixed mentality." According to an examination concentrate via Carol Dweck of Stanford University, a fixed attitude happens when individuals accept fixed qualities that can't change. These individuals archive abilities instead of attempting to foster them. On the other hand, a development attitude accepts that knowledge can develop with time and experience. When individuals accept they can add to their learning, they understand exertion affects their prosperity.

You can attempt to battle a fixed attitude and energize a sound growth mindset by rehearsing the following:

Recognize fixed mindset patterns

To begin with, would you say you are ready to precisely recognize and uncover the negative quirks coming about because of a fixed mentality? Normal practices of these individuals incorporate the individuals who keep away from challenges, surrender effectively, consider there to be as achieving nothing, overlook and keep away from negative criticism, need heading in their objectives, and carry on when feeling undermined by other people who make progress. These are normal signs that employees are battling to see their part in supporting the new turn of events.

Energize feedback over praise

Commendation feels better. We like to feel approved in our qualities and are content to let it be the point at which we get acclaim over achieved work—employees to request input despite the result. There are consistent approaches to improve and create. Lead your group to request tips and innovative manners by which they can move toward new situations.

Pinpoint skills and limitations

Take time out from the ordinary daily schedule to pinpoint your workers' qualities and shortcomings will give an unmistakable beginning stage to an initiative in realizing where holes exist. Have workers independently take strength evaluations and meet with them to go over outcomes. Some may feel compromised and cautious while going over shortcomings, yet having a direct discussion on the finding will prompt better anticipation and recuperating.

Chapter 13:

7 Reasons Why Comparison is The Thief of Joy

Comparison is a poison that creates feelings of jealousy and envy if we do not put reframe our pattern of thought. It is perfectly natural for us to engage in the habit of comparing our lives with those around us even if we had no business to do so.

When we scroll through social media, or hear stories of friends who have bought multi-million dollar properties, it's hard not to look at your own life and wonder what went wrong. Chasing other people's life even though they are not yours can only lead to nowhere.

Today we are going to find out 8 reasons why comparison is the ultimate thief of joy and happiness in our lives.

1. Feelings of Unworthiness

When we engage in comparisons with people who have fancy houses and cars, or those who have very successful careers, especially if they are friends of ours, it is hard not to feel sorry for ourselves. We feel inadequate and lacking. This inferiority complex only serves to remind us that we are lousy and useless, rather than the truth that we are special, unique, and amazing human beings who deserve to be respected and treated the same as people who are 1000x more successful than we are. No amount of success and wealth should make you feel unworthy in the presence of others.

2. We Feel Like We Are Not Where We Should Be

Comparing the amount of stuff and the level of career progression is not something that we should indulge in. That person we are comparing against may have some special talents, are gifted in areas of making money, or whatever reasons that landed them their position today, but that doesn't mean they are better than you. We are all on our own journeys - as long as we are on a path that we have set for ourselves, no matter how unglamorous it is, it is one that we should be proud of.

3. We Constantly Envy Others

Envy is not a good emotion to have, especially if it only makes us bitter at our life circumstances. We start blaming the things around us, our parents, our environment, and so on for the lack of success that we supposedly feel that we should have by now. There will always be someone richer and more successful than you, if you are never happy at where you are, you will never be really happy at all.

4. We Forget How Amazing Our Life Is

Engaging in comparisons is a sure fire way to help us forget how amazing our lives are. Suddenly everything you you own feels like trash next to someone who has something fancier. Your trusty Toyota feels like a garbage vehicle next to a Bentley, your nice condo suddenly feels like a mouse-hole next to that giant bungalow, and your well-to-do income suddenly seems like pocket money next a multi-million dollar earner. Always remind yourself that your life is amazing and that there are people in third world countries who are living life in poverty without proper food and shelter. You are living their dream life.

5. We Try To Force Our Way Into The Life That Others Are Living

By wanting what others have, you may have the tendency to copy their way of life. To try and emulate others, you are abandoning your own beliefs, goals, and dreams, to chase someone else's. You may attempt to climb that same mountain but you may never feel as happy as you are right now doing what you do for a lot less money and stress. People are all wired differently. Some may be workaholics who are able to spend 14 hours a day at the office while not caring about everything else in their life. Are you able to do the same? And are your priorities in life the same as well? If the answer is no, stick to your own path and be happy in it.

6. We Fail To Be Grateful For What We Have

It is perfectly easy to forget how grateful we should be to be alive. That we are born on this earth and we are gifted an opportunity to explore, create, and live. We fail to be grateful for the family and family in our lives, instead looking at the missing pool in our backyard or that extra zero in our bank accounts. Money can be earned and things can be bought, but family and friends only come once in your life. Don't forget you have all these things the next time you compare yourself with someone else.

7. We Are Never At Peace

We all want to have peace of mind. To be able to rest one day on our deathbed and say we have lived a great life. If even in our golden years, we are comparing ourselves with our peers who have achieved fancier things in life, we may only look back in life in regret rather than wonder. Don't waste your time comparing, instead celebrate and live each day in the present.

Conclusion

Focus on yourself. Focus on your journey. Focus on your own path to success. That is the only way forward that you should be striving for. You will be much happier for it. Be thankful that you are able to walk this earth and pursue your dreams. All will fall into place in time. I believe in you.

Chapter 14:

Your Motivational Partner In Life

We all have friends. We all have parents. We may have a partner or other half. We all have teachers.

We love and respect all of them and hopefully, they do too. But have we ever wondered why we do that?

Why do we have to love someone who brought us into this world? Why do we love a person who is not related to us whatsoever, but has a connection with us, and hence we like to hang around them? Why do we respect someone who is being paid to do what makes him respectable?

The answer to all these is simple. They make us a better version of ourselves. Without these people in our lives, we won't be as good as we are right now.

It doesn't matter where we stand right now in our lives, there would always be someone backing you up whenever you feel low.

People tend to seek loneliness and a quiet corner whenever life hits hard. But what they don't realize is that there are people in their lives who have a duty towards you.

Either that be your parents or friends or partner or anyone for that case, you need to find time to give them a chance to show their true affections towards you. You need to give them

Your parents can't give up on you because you are a part of them. You have their legacy to keep and spread. They want you to be a better person than they ever were, hence they will always support you no matter what the world does to you.

Your friends have a bond of loyalty towards you which is the basic root of any friendship. They will always try to help you get up no matter how many times you fall.

All these people owe you this support. And you owe it to them to be a source of inspiration when they want a shoulder to cry. When they want a person to listen and feel their pain. When they need someone to be able to share some time with them without a grain of self-interest.

These things make us stronger as a human and make us grow and evolve as a Specie.

You can find motivation and inspiration from anyone. It may even be a guard in your office or a worker in your office who you might see once a week.

Basic human nature makes us susceptible to the need of finding company. It doesn't matter where it comes from. What you need is a person who can devote a selfless minute of his or her life to you and feels good when they realize they have made a positive change in your life.

Everyone goes through this phase of loneliness but we always find a person who makes us the most comfortable.

The person who reimburses our self-belief. The person who makes us take one more try, one more chance, not for us but for them too. This person is your true motivational partner in life.

Chapter 15:

Five Habits of Permanent Weight Loss

Weight loss is a journey that many people have embarked on. Some of them are doing so out of personal ambition and others out of a doctor's advice. Regardless of their effort, somehow they seem not to be shedding off enough weight. Sometimes, even after losing a substantial amount of weight, they regain it once more and all their effort goes down the drain.

Here are five habits of permanent weight loss:

1. Win Both The Battle and The War

The mind is the arena of the greatest battle. Regardless that weight gain and loss manifests physically, the mind influences greatly on either outcome. When the battle is lost in the mind, the war against weight gain is subsequently lost.

Train your mind in a manner that suits you to be on the winning side. How so? A disciplined mind will win over your body to adhere to a strict routine geared towards weight loss. When you strengthen your mind not to succumb to temptations that will make you lapse in your weight loss journey, you have won half the battle.

As much as you put strategies in place to follow a particular routine, it is bound to fail if you have a weak mindset. No plan you put in place (that of weight loss included) will ever see the light of day when you are mentally unprepared. Similar to how one exercises body muscles, the brain too needs exercise. When your mind can withstand the temptations of eating anything, permanent weight loss is achievable.

2. Seek Professional Help

The best way to solve a problem is to involve experts. Their insight will diagnose the heart of the problem and prescribe a lasting solution. The journey of weight loss gets easier when you follow the advice of medical doctors. You will know what to do not to cause harm to your body.

The ambition of permanent weight loss may get in your way and make you try wild things to achieve your goal. Some people go to the extent of taking herbal concoctions with the belief that it will help them shed some weight. There are instances where these concoctions have caused more harm than the good they intended.

Most people ignore the advice of doctors regarding weight loss. Instead, they prefer some weird prescription of homemade beverages with the hope of permanent weight loss. There is no shortcut to reaching your goal. When you seek professional help regarding how to adjust your lifestyle, you will not lapse back or add extra weight. Permanent weight loss is achievable.

3. Associate With Like-Minded People

It is said that when you want to go fast, go alone but when you want to go far, go with someone. The journey of weight loss is long when you walk alone. Sometimes you may give up on the way and not achieve your goal.

In the company of people with whom you share a common goal – permanent weight loss –, you will encourage each other. In the small circle of friends, you will be able to exchange ideas and strategies for weight loss. This is unachievable when you isolate yourself.

The major challenge that may initially arise is finding the right group of people with whom you share a common goal. In the wrong group, you will be misplaced and permanent weight loss will forever remain a dream. Actualize this dream by excusing yourself from any rudderless group of people.

4. Lifestyle Change

A lifestyle change is a personal decision that one initiates without any external influence whatsoever. It is a conscious decision that one takes while being fully aware of the disruption it may have on his/her life.

Permanent weight loss is possible when one overhauls his/her lifestyle. When you stop taking alcohol or the habit of always driving even over short distances that you could walk, you will start shedding off some weight. Even an innocent habit of sleeping too much during the day will make you add some weight. Avoid it at all costs.

When you do a lifestyle audit and eliminate habits that will work against your goal of weight loss, the destination of permanent weight loss draws nearer. A lifestyle change is a difficult decision but one worth undertaking.

5. Seek Knowledge

Knowledge is power. Seek correct information on weight loss and avoid dwelling on myths, hearsay, and unfounded beliefs. Misinformation and misplacement of facts about weight loss will make it untenable. The fight against weight gain will have a big boost when there are sufficient facts about it.

The goal is not just weight loss but permanent weight loss. How is it achievable if we lack facts about it? Read and consult widely and approach it from a knowledgeable and informed point of view. Do not act blindly on fallacies.

These five habits for permanent weight loss bring significant change when adhered to.

Chapter 16:

Five Habits We Consider

Harmless

Familiarity breeds contempt. There are habits that we have become so accustomed to that hinder us from achieving our full potential. We consider them little and insignificant in our lives. Sometimes, we go to the extremes of defending ourselves when we are corrected and advised to abandon them. It is a sad state to be in and one that requires enlightenment and self-awareness to be able to get out of that quagmire. Here are five habits that we consider harmless:

1. Blue Screen Addiction

Blue screen addiction is the addiction to digital media and video games. This is a common problem, especially for millennials. It is often considered inconsequential, a myth that has been debunked by real-life experiences.

Most people spend a lot of time working through their computers, using their mobile phones or tablets, playing video games, or watching television. The use of digital media in this era is almost unavoidable. Regardless of this digital evolution, there have been some excesses. Heavy use of these devices has broken the social code since most people can only communicate through communication apps and not physically.

Faceless cyberbullies have attacked and trolled innocent netizens and ruined their reputation.

News spread fast via the internet and it is not a surprise that addiction to blue screens is on the rise. It is not as harmless as it may seem and its effects are long-lasting. It causes poor eyesight and sometimes migraines.

2. Procrastination

It is the habit of postponing tasks to be done presently to a later time. Most people relate to this habit that has grown roots in our lifestyle. Before you judge yourself harshly for doing this, statistics have it that over 80% of college students engage in procrastination and it has chronically affected at least 20% of adults. That is just the tip of the iceberg.

We comfort ourselves that we are not alone in this ocean that has drowned the ambitions and potential of many people. We err in finding comfort in this well-dressed misery of procrastination. It is not as harmless as it superficially looks.

Procrastination encourages laziness which has, in turn, made many people pay a higher price for engaging in it. Some have lost their employment for leaving incomplete tasks at work, others have missed out on promotions for incompetence and a further group has failed to secure business opportunities that required their attention at the opportune time when they had put everything on hold. What is the cost we are ready to pay for in procrastination?

We should sober up and abandon procrastination by acting on matters that need our immediate attention. Shelving our response for a later time causes more harm than good.

3. Making Obnoxious Jokes

There is a limit to the extreme one can go when making jokes. It should never go overboard to hurt the feelings of our friends and associates. Many times we underestimate or maybe do not consider the impact our words may have on our friends and those around us. We unknowingly hurt their self-esteem and they feel worthless after what turns out to be a bad joke. We should always know when to stop and apologize for our excesses because we never know how much we have hurt our friends when we make bad jokes about them.

It is inconsiderate of us not to take into account the struggles of our friends when we make fun of their situation. It seems harmless but has the potential to completely cut off one's dreams.

4. Building A Fortress

The single greatest mistake that we unknowingly commit is building a fortress for ourselves to hide from the rest of the world. Indeed, the world can sometimes be cruel and unforgiving, making us run to the nearest point of safety. We build walls instead of bridges to separate us from the harsh reality. This solution is short-lived because the fortress will cut you off from the rest of the world.

You will live in solitude without any news and over time your resources will be depleted. The fortress may not necessarily be physical but also social. As much as introverts manage to keep off squabbles and fights, they lack a network to connect. It is not safe to be alone in this ever-changing world. Find a person or group with whom you share common interests and build a network.

Your network is your net worth.

5. Glossing Over Facts

Facts should be the language you speak. We often omit or ignore facts that we deem irrelevant to us but surprisingly turn out to be very important. When you get your facts right, everything falls into place. Often, the average person does not go into the details. Remember the devil lies in the details? It is therein where you will find solutions to matters that you overlooked.

Stand out by grasping correct facts about a matter before you indulge in them. It is harmful not to be aware of your surroundings or get your facts right because it puts your competence on the relevant subject matter in question.

You should check out these five habits that we mistakenly consider harmless and adjust your approach.

Chapter 17:

Happy People Savor the Moment

Learning to "savor the moment" in life is a convenient, free, and effective way to increase your happiness and quality of life and reduce stress. Enjoying what you have can help you to appreciate what you've got rather than lamenting what you don't have and creating stress by striving for too much. Being able to savor the moment with loved ones can bring a stronger connection and sense of appreciation, which leads to better quality relationships and all the benefits of social support that they bring. Learn more about these techniques to savor the moment in life.

1. Focus on Details

Sometimes as we go through life, we forget to stop and enjoy the little things; indeed, it's possible to go through an entire day either stuck in your ruminations about the past or anxious over the future, never really seizing the moment and noticing the pleasant things that are happening right now (and passing up positive opportunities right and left). As you savor the moment, notice the little things that can make a day special — the smile of a friend, the kindness of a stranger, the beauty of a sunset

2. Focus on Sensations

As you're experiencing your day, notice and memorize the details — especially the positive details — of what's happening around you. Create a memory. Notice the sounds you hear, like the sound of children's laughter in the background. Notice the smells, like the scent of a fresh sea breeze. And how did that wind feel on your face? Noticing these types of sensory details helps you live fully in the moment and can help evoke pleasant memories when you hear music, smell aroma, or feel sensations you experience on the days you want to savor.

3. Focus on the Positive

As humans, we're naturally wired to notice the negative events in life more than the positive, as these are what we need to keep track of to maintain our safety: if we're aware of threats around us, we're more able to launch a defense. However, if we actively focus on the positive, we can stress less and enjoy life more from an increasingly optimistic vantage point. To savor the moment, notice what's going right, and appreciate it. This isn't the same as pretending you're happy when you're not; it's more about noticing the things that lead to greater happiness and reduced stress.

4. Express Gratitude

Feeling gratitude goes along with noticing the positive and is an excellent way to savor the moment. Notice all the nice things that people do for you (and thank them whenever possible), or simply notice what you enjoy about people when they're just themselves (and be sure to tell them that, too). Appreciate what goes right in your day as it happens, and write it down in a gratitude journal at night — it's a surprisingly effective way to both raise your level of daily gratitude and build a record of all the things in your life that can make you happy when you're having a bad day.

Chapter 18:

How To Be A Better Listener

Today we're going to talk about a topic that could potentially help you not only in your relationships, such as with your boyfriend, girlfriend, and best friends, but also in your workplace with your colleagues, peers, and your bosses or understudies.

Why is being a better listener so vital you might ask? It is simple, because as humans, we all want to be heard. And we all want to feel like people are listening to us and understanding us not just on a superficial level, but emotionally as well. We have a desire to share our pains, sorrows, unhappiness, and even happiness and special events with people who are willing to lend a listening ear to us. And we instantly feel connected to the person who is listening to us.

We are given a mouth and two ears for a reason. I know it sounds silly, but I have to repeat again here that we are social creatures, and we try to find connections with people as much as we can. And there is no better way to be connected than with someone who are willing to spend the time to hear us.

Think back to a time when someone actually told u, thanks for listening to my problems. Either through text or in person. How did you feel? And how did they react to you being a good listener? Were they appreciative? Or were they nonchalant about it. I would bet that they were appreciative and they know that they had found someone that they could count on to tell their problems too. Of course u dont want it to be a habit that someone constantly "bitches" to you about every single thing that is going wrong in their life. You have to learn how to draw the line there. But generally if it is a one-off problem, I'm sure you guys became better friends, partners, or lovers.

Now think back to a time when someone told u off for not listening to their problems. Where you constantly interjected their sharing with advice without letting them finish what they had to say. This would most likely be your partner who would get angry at you, but what were their feelings at that point? Did they say "you're not listening to me" or "You dont understand?". That has happened to me before on multiple occasions when i tried to impose my ideas on a situation thinking that that is what the person wanted, advice. But in reality, they know how to solve the problem but they just want someone that they could vent to. To share their story and then move on.

So if people have been telling u that you're not a good listener, or that you don't listen or that u dont understand what they want, more often than not, the problem is that you did not just let the person say what they wanted to say, to have their piece. Your job is not to dish out advice, but just to sit there, interested, and ask them to go on. And at the end of it give out a hug rather than an advice.

So you must be wondering how this could link to your colleagues. Well for one, you have to be a good person to begin with in order for people to trust u with work related matters. If colleagues don't trust you, they won't be open to sharing with you problems they might have with their bosses or other issues that they need to vent about. But if they do trust you, and know you are not the type who will go round spreading gossip but rather is a good genuine person with a good heart and a listening ear, you have just gotten yourself an ally at the workplace. And you would have built a friendship at work that could last you a lifetime. You never know when these connections that you have made would provide you with future job opportunities, whether these colleagues could become your bosses in another company one day. But you want to keep your colleagues close to you and you want to retain their respect, trust, and be professional. Vice versa, you may also find a listening ear in a colleague that you can share your problems with. But i must warn you that sometimes people can be disingenuous so you've gotta be careful to not overshare information that could be used against you. Especially through messages where they can be screen captured and could get you in trouble.

On the flip side, Now I want you to use this power for good and not as insider information to manipulate your way up to corporate ladder, do what you will with your gift but karma does come around. And if you have ill intentions for being a good listener, it will come back to bite you someday. I am certain of it. People will know you are a faker and your reputation will precede you.

As you can clearly, being a good listener has immense pay offs for your personal and professional career. And learning to have an open ear could help you gain many potential friends at work and at play. How you respond when people share their stories and having a good character yourself personally also plays an important role in actually keeping these friends close to you as well, but being a good listener is a nice way to start.

Chapter 19:

Happy People Take Care of Themselves

I frequently hear the word "selfish" tossed about in coaching, often with a negative connotation. Someone feels bad that they were selfish or that someone else was selfish, and it was offensive. Selfishness – the lack of considering others or only being concerned with your advantage – can be a great weakness. The ability to put others' needs in front of your own is an important life skill that you need to be able to do without resentment, even when it's completely inconvenient and a sacrifice.

However, I would argue that the motivation behind that decision should be self-serving. In most cases, being selfish is just a matter of perspective, critical to happiness and self-evolution.

Let me explain…

First, let's talk about why it is so important to be selfish. As author Brené Brown has discovered in her research on wholehearted living, loving yourself more than you love others is the first and most critical step to seeking happiness and fulfillment.

She says it is impossible to love anyone more than you love yourself. Taking care of yourself is the pathway to fulfillment and high performance in work and life. And, just as importantly, it's a gift to others.

When your needs are met, and you feel good about yourself, it's easier to elevate other people's needs in front of your own. It's easy to be a giver when your cup is full. When you feel half-full or empty, it's harder to give. You inherently feel people should be giving more to you or others, so you don't have to give so much or feel you need to preserve more for yourself.

Here are the two common derailments that can prevent you from finding fulfillment:

1. Giving too much

When people give too much - continually put other people's needs ahead of their own - builds resentment and takes away from their ability to take care of themselves. When their time is so focused on others, they don't have any time left for themselves. I find people do this when they are uncomfortable asking for their needs, speaking up about issues, or delegating responsibilities. Often they hide these weaknesses by focusing on other people, so they don't have to focus on themselves. This not only leads to feeling unfulfilled but becomes a burden on others who feel they need to take care of the "giver."

2. Taking too much time for ourselves

On the opposite end of the spectrum, some people take too much time for themselves, mistakenly thinking it will lead to fulfillment. They do not "give" enough, and it usually makes them feel worse, disengaging them from relationships and putting them on a treadmill of trying to do something that will finally make them feel good. In these cases, they are usually working on the wrong issues. The places where they are investing their time do not give them meaning.

Chapter 20:

Happy People Spend Time Alone

No man is an island except for similarly as we blossom with human contact and connections, so too would we be able to prosper from time burned through alone. Also, this, maybe, turns out to be particularly important right now since we're all in detachment. We've since quite a while ago slandered the individuals who decide to be distant from everyone else, except isolation shouldn't be mistaken for forlornness. Here are two mental reasons why investing energy in isolation makes us more joyful and more satisfied:

1. Spending time alone reconnects us.

Our inclination for isolation might be transformative, as indicated by an examination distributed in the British Journal of Psychology in 2016. Utilizing what they call "the Savannah hypothesis of satisfaction," transformative clinicians Satoshi Kanazawa of the London School of Economics and Norman Li of Singapore Management University accept that the single, tracker accumulate way of life of our precursors structure the establishment of what satisfies us in present-day times. The group examined a study of 15,000 individuals matured somewhere between 18 and 28 in the United States. They found that individuals living in more thickly populated regions were fundamentally less cheerful than the individuals who lived in more modest networks.

"The higher the populace thickness of the prompt climate, the less glad" respondents were. The scientists accept this is because we had advanced mentally from when mankind, for the most part, existed on distant, open savannahs. Since quite a while ago, we have instilled an inclination to be content alone, albeit current life generally neutralizes that. Also, as good to beat all, they tracked down that the more clever an individual was, the more they appreciated investing energy alone. Along these lines, isolation makes you more joyful AND is evidence of your smarts. We're in.

2. Spending Time Alone Teaches Us Empathy

Investing in a specific measure of energy alone can create more compassion towards others than a milestone concentrate from Harvard. Scientists found that when enormous gatherings of individuals encircle us, it's harder for us to acquire viewpoints and tune into the sensations of others. However, when we venture outside that unique circumstance, the extra headspace implies we can feel for the situation of individuals around us in a more genuine and significant manner. Furthermore, that is uplifting news for others, but different investigations show that compassion and helping other people are significant to prosperity and individual satisfaction.

"At the point when you invest energy with a specific friend network or your colleagues, you foster a 'we versus them' attitude," clarifies psychotherapist and creator Amy Morin. "Investing energy alone assists you with growing more empathy for individuals who may not find a way into your 'inward circle.' "On the off chance that you're not used to isolation, it can feel awkward from the outset," she adds. "However, making that tranquil time for yourself could be critical to turning into the best form of yourself."

Chapter 21:

Things That Steal Your Motivation

Motivation seems a common word, sometimes a bit overrated. But it matters to those who haven't had one good moment for a long time.

The person who has everything might not like to talk about motivation. But the person who struggles and after some time gives up needs some motivation to keep going and keep doing so that he has something to achieve and live for.

Motivation is central to a good and productive life but most people lose it too soon. Some know how to regain it but some don't have a single clue what got them distracted.

Fear is a generic flaw in every human's life. People tend to fear the simplest of things and the simplest of feelings. Some call it a phobia, some call it hesitation or someone might call it smart planning.

The fact is that you don't have what it takes to do what you are reluctant to do. It may be due to fear of failure or fear of getting laughed at.

Fear keeps you from trying things that are easy to excel at and require absolutely no effort rather determination, and taking away one's determination is the direct path to demotivation

You fear something so you avoid taking a step and hence you lack the hard work that is elementary to everything in life.

Not working to your full potential is another thing that keeps the best outcomes at bay. The outcomes might surprise you and might motivate you to work even harder for the diamonds that lie ahead.

The thing that made us evolve as a human and has lead to all things we have achieved till now is competition. The competition requires us to compare our present to someone better than us and this comparison doesn't always work well for us.

We have to accept the fact that there are people more deserving and more achieved than us. But these feelings shouldn't keep us lying around and not doing to get to that place too. We have everything in life if we have a healthy body and air in our lungs. What you need more is a little motivation to get closer to the ones you idealize.

This Inferiority complex makes us wait for something to happen on its own. But what you should be doing is to get up, tie those shoes and run towards what you want. You cannot expect something to be served to you with you sitting there all day.

Chances don't come in a lottery. Fortune favors those who take risks and want to create chances. Even if you miss one chance, don't take it hard on yourself. You don't need to condemn yourself for one lost chance unless you have the same attitude when the next chance comes knocking around.

Motivation isn't a lost cause till you haven't knocked on all doors. When you have no doubts remaining, you will be successful on every next step.

Chapter 22:

Happy People Find Reasons to Laugh and Forge Deep Connections

"…Making a connection with men and women through humour, happiness and laughter not only helps you make new friends, but it is the means to establish a strong, meaningful connection to people."

People always try to have a personality that attracts people and makes them feel comfortable around them. Utilizing their humour has been one of those ways to create new friendships. But once you start doing this, you will realize that this humorous nature has emotions and attitudes that comprise happiness and positivity. This will also help you create deep and meaningful connections that will last a lifetime.

When you intend to focus on humour to find deep connections, your subconscious mind starts focusing on positivity. You will slowly turn out to be more positive in your reasoning and conduct because awareness of what's funny is truly only demonstrative of one's very own bliss. In this manner, you're sustaining a more appealing, and that's just the beginning "contagious" attitude. Similarly, as we search out bliss in our everyday lives through satisfying work, leisure activities, individual interests and day to day life, so too do people seek out and wish to be encircled by joy on a relational level: joy and bitterness are contagious, and we as a whole wish to get the happy bug.

Humour helps fashion friendships since we wish to encircle ourselves with individuals who are glad. This way, our objective shouldn't just be to utilize humour to make new companions, however to zero in on the entirety of the uplifting perspectives and feelings that include an entertaining and carefree nature. By embodying satisfaction, inspiration, happiness, receptiveness and tranquillity, we sustain a more grounded and "contagious" state of being.

Historically there was a negative connotation attached to humour, but over the years, research was done, and it proved otherwise. In any case, research on humour has come into the daylight, with humour currently seen as a character strength. Good brain science, a field that analyzes what individuals progress admirably, notes that humour can be utilized to cause others to feel better, acquire closeness, or help buffer pressure. Alongside appreciation, expectation and otherworldliness, a funny bone has a place with the arrangement of qualities positive clinicians call greatness; together, they help us manufacture associations with the world and give significance to life. Enthusiasm for humour corresponds with different qualities, as well, like insight and love of learning. Furthermore, humour exercises or activities bring about expanded sensations of passionate prosperity and idealism.

Once you step into adulthood, it can be difficult for many people to form friendships and then keep up with them because all of us get busier in our lives. Still, it's never too much to go to a bar and strike up a conversation with a random person and believe us, if you have a good sense of humour, they will be naturally attracted towards you.

Chapter 23:

10 Habits of Katy Perry

If pop music is your kind of music, then you've probably heard of Katy Perry, the best-selling pop artist in the mid-2000s. Katy Perry is an American singer, songwriter, and reality T.V. show, judge. The star is well-known for her countless smash hits like 'I Kissed a Girl,' 'Teenage Dream,' 'Firework,' and 'Dark Horse,' memorable performances, and a unique onstage persona.

Katy began her career with a gospel album before transitioning to pop music. She has won several awards, sold over 18 million records worldwide, and was named one of the highest-earning women in the music industry between 2011 and 2018. Curious about how she reached here? Well, you're not alone.

Here are the 10 habits of Katy Perry.

1. Focus on Being the First Great You

When Katy first got her way to Hollywood, record agents and producers told her, "you're the next Brittany Spears! You're Avril Lavigne's replacement! Ashley Simpson in the making!" What was Katy's reaction? Excited? NO! She made it clear that she would rather be the original Katy Perry. So, whose shadow do you live in?

2. Success Typically Takes Years

Katy's success story is not an overnight thing. She went through unsuccessful agencies, record labels, and producers. Most of all, she had to work on her personality, style up, and enhance her sound. Intriguing, she didn't give; you can see how great she turned to be. It isn't a competition. If you're on the right track, stick with it.

3. Sleep Is Key

Perry understands the essence of having an adequate sleep. She told Glamour that ten hours' sleep is something not taken for granted. She spends an hour and a half on the elliptical machine and yoga; soon, she wakes up. If you get enough sleep, you can't get the energy to be productive throughout the day.

4. Allow Yourself Time To Unwind

Perry told Cleo Wade in an interview that her new year's resolutions are always to switch off her phone one day a week. Every day, the singer spends an hour of transcendental meditation on reconnecting with reality and disengaging from the internet. It's all goes to your mental health, relaxation, eat well, and workout.

5. The Show Must Continue

Katy is the epitome of strength, elegance, and composure. There was a moment she was going through a divorce and still expected to perform for fans who were out there mesmerized by her presence. She did, however, take the stage and outdid herself. You know how it feels when everything around you is falling apart, and all you want to do is cuddle up and cry, but the show must go on.

6. Stay Confident

According to the star, when you confidently present yourself, you'll pull off anything. And the more you believe in yourself, the better your chances of success. There is no doubt that Katy Perry is a much confident person, from her stage presence, style, the way she behaves in public and with fans to her exuding confidence after making mistakes.

7. Own Your Mistakes

Katy's 2017 public apology for being cultural appropriation after appearing like a geisha at the 2013 American Music Awards and sporting cornrows in the 2014 video for "This Is How We Do," and recently burying the hatch with her fellow pop singer Taylor Swift, are good examples of being remorseful. Own up, and learn from your mistakes.

8. Stay True to Yourself

Being raised in a strict, religious household, you're probably ousted from indulging in secular music, media, mainstream, and the outside influence. That's Katy Perry! However, despite her parents' attempt to allure her in making gospel music, she went her way to pursue pop music. It was a rough patch, but she smashed it. Just stay true to yourself as you work through your goals.

9. Reinvent Constantly

Judging from Perry's sound modification over time, it's worth saying that when you constantly reinvent your craft, you'll not only grow but also will achieve greatness. Katy is well-known for her light pop tunes, yet she isn't hesitant to take chances on songs like "E.T." and "Dark Horse." She also has a penchant for creating emotionally laden songs such as "Unconditionally" and "The One That Got Away."

10. Takes On New Opportunities

Yes, you probably know Perry as a pop sensation, but were you prepared for her to take over the world's T.V. reality realm? Perry relaunched her career as a judge on the famous ABC edition of American Idol, where she shared the stage with Luke Bryan and Lionel Ritchie, a move that not only boosted her latest album but also boosted her stardom.

Conclusion

Allowing a string of failures to deter you from following your dreams is a definite setback. Katy's more unsuccessful years may have boosted her growth into the record-breaking artist she is known for today. Keep learning, grow, and, most importantly, persevere.

Chapter 24:

Happy People Use Their Character Strengths

One of the most popular exercises in the science of positive psychology (some argue it is the single most popular exercise) is referred to as "use your signature strengths in new ways." But what does this exercise mean? How do you make the most of it to benefit yourself and others?

On the surface, the exercise is self-explanatory:

a. Select one of your highest strengths – one of your **character strengths** that is core to who you are, is easy for you to use, and gives you energy;

b. Consider a new way to express the strength each day;

c. Express the strength in a new way each day for at least 1 week.

Studies repeatedly show that this exercise is connected with long-term benefits (e.g., 6 months) such as higher levels of happiness and lower levels of depression.

PUT THE EXERCISE INTO PRACTICE

In practice, however, people sometimes find it surprisingly challenging to come up with new ways to use one of their signature strengths. This is because we are very accustomed to using our strengths. We frequently use our strengths mindlessly without much awareness. For example, have you paid much attention to your use of self-regulation as you brush your teeth? Your level of prudence or kindness while driving? Your humility while at a team meeting?

For some strengths, it is easy to come up with examples. Want to apply **curiosity** in a new way? Below is a sample mapping of what you might do. Keep it simple. Make it complex. It's up to you!

- On Monday, take a new route home from work and explore your environment as you drive.
- On Tuesday, ask one of your co-workers a question you have not previously asked them.
- On Wednesday, try a new food for lunch – something that piques your curiosity to taste.
- On Thursday, call a family member and explore their feelings about a recent positive experience they had.
- On Friday, take the stairs instead of the elevator and explore the environment as you do.
- On Saturday, as you do one household chore (e.g., washing the dishes, vacuuming), pay attention to 3 novel features of the activity while you do it. Example: Notice the whirring sound of the vacuum, the accumulation of dust swirling around in the container, the warmth of the water as you wash the dishes, the sensation of the weight of a single plate or cup, and so on.
- On Sunday, ask yourself 2 questions you want to explore about yourself – reflect or journal your immediate responses.
- Next Monday….keep going!

WIDENING THE SCOPE

In some instances, you might feel challenged to come up with examples. Let me help. After you choose one of your signature strengths, consider the following 10 areas to help jolt new ideas within you and stretch your approach to the strength.

How might I express the character strength...

- At work
- In my closest relationship
- While I engage in a hobby
- When with my friends
- When with my parents or children
- When I am alone at home
- When I am on a team
- As the leader of a project or group
- While I am driving
- While I am eating

Chapter 25:

10 Habits of Meryl Streep

Meryl Streep is an American actress known for her incomparable abilities; she can adapt to complicated accents, sing, be a comedian, and play old male rabbi. Meryl roles have brought her from African bush and Greece beaches, Julia Child's legendary kitchen, and Disney wonderland. If you have watched Meryl ace her roles, this doesn't sound like a standard joke. Meryl is undoubtedly a Hollywood queen with 21 Academy Award nominations and three wins for Kramer vs. Kramer, Sophie's Choice, and The Iron Lady. Rising to such fame, staying modest and brilliant, and, ahem-an an estimation of $ 160 million net-worth, Meryl maintains specific principles.

Here are 10 habits of Meryl Streep to enumerate from.

1. Focus on the Skills Rather Than Looks

During an interview with Vogue, Meryl said that stressing about your weight or skin will derail you. Instead, concentrate on what you enjoy doing, as what you put your hands on should be your world. Meryl had repeatedly reiterated her stance on choosing genius over beauty, even when told she is "too ugly."

2. Focus on the Bigger Picture

It is natural for people to succumb to the muck of stress, deadlines, and anxiety. It is also common to find yourself overcommitting or doubting whether you can do a task or achieve a specific goal. However, if you take a step back and breathe, you will see the bigger picture. Meryl said that the one thing she could tell her 20-something old self would be to think big. She wished she could have devoted more time comprehending the critical role she had in society.

3. Be Authentic

Never, ever apologize for being true to yourself. Meryl was called fat, ugly, and her nose being ridiculed. She recalls how at first, her self-esteem declined to a point she couldn't even watch her shows but later made it her aim to criticize societal expectations of a slim, perfect, and beautiful goddess Hollywood queen.

4. Listen Always

Meryl studies accents as well as what they communicate to stay in tune with the roles she portrays. She achieves this by empathically listening. It means listening before and after work and in between work-to those you associate daily to learn, listening to everything.

5. Age Is Just a Number

Meryl insists on embracing your age and doing what you can utmost at any phase. She has always been vocal against Hollywood manifestations of stripping female actresses short. Meryl has used her influence to fight against ageism, demonstrating that women of all ages deserve to be heard, seen, and appreciated.

6. Start by Starting, Stay Consistent

In the 90s, Meryl kept on making moves despite getting zero Oscar nominations. You have to keep doing what you're doing. Just keep going no matter what.

7. Stay Connected With Your Family

If you are a mother and jogs between 8 to 10 working hours and attending to your family, you hold a soft spot in Meryl's heart. In a podcast, she recounts how her priority was only on those roles that were both location and time-friendly to have quality time with her family.

8. Make the Mold, Then Advance It

After developing an understanding of yourself, set your standards and navigate your way through, which you'll rely on. It is about what feels suitable to you, not what you've been told. Throughout her 45-year career, Meryl has created and reinvented herself, thus ensuring that she improves her talent, craft, and ideas and remaining relevant in Hollywood.

9. Good Things Take Time

In modern society, delayed progress is no progress, and the patient feels worthless than virtuous. Nonetheless, Meryl's career journey is an excellent example of how good things take time because it wasn't until 10 years after acting that she gained the recognition she deserved. Persist at it until you get to where you want to be.

10. Stay Humble

Meryl Streep often referred to as the best actress of her generation, would have within her rights succumbed to the luxuries of being a celebrity. But she chose to stay grounded, and as she told Vogue Magazine that she tried as much to live an ordinary life as when you do your own taming, you cannot get spoilt.

Conclusion

Having has built a successful career from the bottom through her appearances and roles in films and other avenues, Meryl Strip has become an iconic influence that seamlessly defines how you can hit the top by just being you.

Chapter 26:

How to Love Yourself First

It's so easy to tell someone "Love yourself" and much more difficult to describe *how* to do it. Learn and practice these six steps to gradually start loving yourself more every day:

Step 1: Be willing to feel pain and take responsibility for your feelings.

Step 1 is mindfully following your breath to become present in your body and embrace all of your feelings. It's about moving toward your feelings rather than running away from them with various forms of self-abandonment, such as staying focused in your head, judging yourself, turning to addictions to numb out, etc. All feelings are informational.

Step 2: Move into the intent to learn.

Commit to learning about your emotions, even the ones that may be causing you pain, so that you can move into taking loving action.

Step 3: Learn about your false beliefs.

Step 3 is a deep and compassionate process of exploration—learning about your beliefs and behavior and what is happening with a person or situation that may be causing your pain. Ask your feeling self, your inner child: "What am I thinking or doing that's causing the painful feelings of anxiety, depression, guilt, shame, jealousy, anger, loneliness, or emptiness?" Allow the answer to come from inside, from your intuition and feelings.

Once you understand what you're thinking or doing that's causing these feelings, ask your ego about the fears and false beliefs leading to the self-abandoning thoughts and actions.

Step 4: Start a dialogue with your higher self.

It's not as hard to connect with your higher guidance as you may think. The key is to be open to learning about loving yourself. The answers may come immediately or over time. They may come in words or images or dreams. When your heart is open to learning, the answers will come.

Step 5: Take loving action.

Sometimes people think of "loving myself" as a feeling to be conjured up. A good way to look at loving yourself is by emphasizing the action: "What can I *do* to love myself?" rather than "How can I *feel* love for myself?"

By this point, you've already opened up to your pain, moved into learning, started a dialogue with your feelings, and tapped into your spiritual guidance. Step 5 involves taking one of the loving actions you identified in Step 4. However small they may seem at first, over time, these actions add up.

Step 6: Evaluate your action and begin again as needed.

Once you take the loving action, check in to see if your pain, anger, and shame are getting healed. If not, you go back through the steps until you discover the truth and loving actions that bring you peace, joy, and a deep sense of intrinsic worth.

Over time, you will discover that loving yourself improves everything in your life—your relationships, health and well-being, ability to manifest your dreams, and self-esteem. Loving and connecting with yourself is the key to loving and connecting with others and creating loving relationships. Loving yourself is the key to creating a passionate, fulfilled, and joyful life.

Chapter 27:

10 Habits of Nancy Pelosi

You can't acknowledge prominent women in the history of American politics without mentioning Nancy Pelosi. Nancy Pelosi is a well-known American politician and a Democrat. She is the current Speaker of the House of representatives for yet another term under President Biden's administration-which marks nearly 50-years in politics.

Pelosi began her political journey in 1976 when she was elected to the Democratic Party National Committee. In 1977, she rose to become the party's leader in California. Pelosi has held the positions of Minority Whip and Minority Leader. Curious of how she rose to such prominence?

Here are 10 Habits of Nancy Pelosi.

1. Establish and Pursue Your Dreams

According to Pelosi, you can't succeed in life without a clear vision and willingness to pursue it. Looking at her political career journey, it's evidence that she has achieved what she desired as a successful politician. Pelosi noted in an interview that you would fail to realize your goals if your focus is on things that don't align with your desires.

2. It Doesn't Matter What Gender You Are

Pelosi believes that it makes no difference whether you are a man or a woman; as long as you have the necessary skills, you can flourish in any role. She urges women to be courageous enough to challenge the notion of "male dominated roles." Pelosi joined politics when patriarchy was at its core and later became the first female Speaker of the House of Representatives.

3. Work Collaboratively With Others

Pelosi acknowledges the essence of working with other people who has the same affiliation as you-in this case, her democrat party members. To achieve great things, you will need the help and input of others, particularly those with more skills and experience. However, it would be best if you only worked with those who believe in you.

4. Be Your Own Best Sensationalist

Self-promotion is something frowned about, but someone has to do it. Do you know who doesn't hold back when it comes to bragging about how terrific she is? Pelosi herself. At a press conference in 2017, Pelosi flaunted how she was a master legislator, strategic, politically adept leader, among others. If you don't publicize yourself out there, who will?

5. Enjoy the Fight

There are two-way contented warriors in DC, and then there is Nancy Pelosi. In an interview, when asked to respond to Dianne Feinstein's statement that women in politics should be prepared to take a punch, she responded with a broad smile, "you must also know how to throw it too."

6. Keep Your Frenemies Closer

According to Pelosi, keep your frenemies closer enough to cooperate with when necessary. However, there is a dark, cold place for democrats like Rep. Moulton for his efforts to oust Pelosi earlier in 2018. "What do you call someone who seems 99% loyal? Disloyal!" In short, if you're going after Pelosi, you better win.

7. Be True to Your Authentic Self

When should you change your mind, and when should you stick to your guns? The answer to that all-time leadership question is not only "it depends," but also when it's right in the eyes of the public. Nancy demonstrates as she puts it, "sticking to your guns and not succumbing to needless pressure."

8. Money Talks

Money is power in politics and business; you must master the money game, as Pelosi has. Her political career has been defined by fundraising, both for her party and for individual candidates too. This is how you win hearts and list up your political allies.

9. Claim Your Place at the Table

Having spent years paddling up the ladder, expect no rush in endorsing Pelosi's replacement. As Molly Ball's book, "Pelosi" indicates, calling herself a "transitional leader" merely meant that those who wished to limit her term were naive. Did it just prove true? She exemplifies what it looks like when a woman doesn't care what other people think or call her—as long as you call her "madam speaker" one more time.

10. Leadership Is About Personal Experience

Consider this: politicians and toddlers have a lot in common, don't they? For Pelosi, having a large family and a leader necessitates being efficient with your time and getting things done. And also being patient enough when dealing with people who can throw tantrums and need to be taken care of.

Conclusion

Strong, powerful women like Nancy Pelosi demonstrates the importance of women's involvement in political processes. As a woman, embrace your power and value your experience enough to conquer a political battle that men take privilege in.

Chapter 28:

Happy People Do What Matters to Them

Think about what you want most out of life. What were you created for? What is your mission in life? What is your passion? You were put on this earth for a reason, and knowing that reason will help you determine your priorities.

I spent a total of four months in the hospital, healing from my sickness. During that time, I spent a lot of time thinking about my purpose in life. I discovered that my purpose is to help you change your lives by focusing on what matters most to you.

1. Create A Plan

Create a plan to get from where you are today to where you want to be. Maybe you need a new job. Maybe you need to go back to school. Maybe you need to deal with some relationship issues. Whatever it is, create a plan that will get you to where you want to be.

While I was in the hospital, I began to draft my life plan. My plan guides all of my actions, helps me focus on my relationships with my wife and daughter, and helps me keep working toward my life purpose. A life plan will help you focus your life too.

2. Focus On Now

Stop multitasking and focus on one thing at a time. It may be a project at work. It may be a conversation with your best friend. It may just be the book that you have wanted to read for months. The key is to focus on one thing at a time.

I plan each day the night before by picking the three most important tasks from my to-do list. In the morning, I focus on each one of these tasks individually until they are completed. Once I complete these three tasks, I check email, return phone calls, etc.

3. Just Say "No."

We all have too much to do and too little time. The only way you will find the time for the things that matter is to say "no" to the things that don't.

I use my purpose and life plan to make decisions about the projects and tasks I say yes to. If a project or task is not aligned with my purpose, a good fit with my life plan, and sometimes that I have time to accomplish, I say no to the project. Saying no to good opportunities gives you time to focus on the best opportunities.

Research tells us that 97 percent of people are living their life by default and not by design. They don't know where their life is headed and don't plan what they want to accomplish in life.

These steps will help you to decide what matters most to you. They will help you to begin living your life by design and not by default. Most importantly, they will help you to create a life focused on what matters to you.

Let me end by asking, "What matters most to you?

Chapter 29:

10 Habits of Jennifer Lawrence

Jennifer Lawrence is one of Hollywood's most famous actress, thanks to her role in films such as "The Hunger Games" and "Silver Linings Playbook." But, before her tremendous success, Lawrence struggled to build a name for herself as an actress and model in New York, where she moved when she was 14 years old. After breaking out as the tough-as-nails teenager Ree in the 2010 indie drama "Winter's Bone," Lawrence went on to star in multiple "X-Men" films and drama such as "American Hustle."

I can't think of anyone who doesn't adore Jennifer Lawrence. What is it about this actress that makes her so appealing? It's easy to list a thousand reasons to admire Jennifer Lawrence -from her incredible skill to her quick-witted humour- but honestly, the life lessons she attracts everyone to her.

Here are 10 life habits that Lawrence offers as lessons simply by being herself.

1. Strive for Health and Strength

"I'm never going to starve myself for a part," she declared on the cover of Elle in December 2012. "I don't want little girls to think, 'Oh, I want to look like Katniss; hence I'll skip meals." When you're trying to get your physique to appear just suitable, Emma on the other end is trying to make her body appear muscular and robust rather than skinny.

2. Refresh Yourself

How many times has Lawrence stumbled? That's what probably comes to your mind every time you see her trip over the hem of her gown at an awards presentation. Can anyone blame the girl for this? Those outfits appear to be impossible to walk in! But she trips, and every time, without fail, she gets back up and continues walking.

3. Accept Responsibility for Your Mistakes

Lawrence's awkward moments are all the more endearing because she is always the first to laugh at how clumsy she is when she stands. Remember when she collapsed at the 2013 Academy Awards? Or when she collapsed on the red carpet of the 2014 Academy Awards? What does it matter? We're all human, and J. Law never tries to hide it by acting cool and so should you.

4. The Truth Will Set You Free

Even if your truth seems to hurt more, such as that you pee very quickly or that your breasts are unequal, J. Law says that it is what it is, and to be anything other than herself isn't allowed. Embrace your flaws!

5. Look Past the Hype

Remember to key in what's genuine and what's not, and to keep your things in perspective, look past those who take themselves too seriously.

6. Maintain An Open Mind

Lawrence told E! News that her acting job will not bind her for the rest of her life. However, she understands that things happen and that people's lives change, and she is prepared to keep an open mind about it. Being open-minded will direct you to break the monotony for future possibilities.

7. Nobody Is Flawless

Can you recall a scene in American Hustle in which Lawrence's character discusses nail polish? Do you remember the nail polish? She claims it's the smell that keeps drawing her back since it's delicious on the outside but rotten on the inside. Not only is it a beautiful moment, but the discussion is a metaphor for everyone's good and evil sides. Nobody is flawless, and no one loves it when others claim to be.

8. Humility

During a BBC Radio 1 interview, Lawrence remarked her involvement in "The Hunger Games," where she genuinely adores watching the movies she makes because she gets to see how much of a troll, bad, and untalented is. Weird! Indeed, you wouldn't agree with her right? Bu she's adorable because she is humble.

9. Maintain a Sense of Humour

During an interview with Vogue, Lawrence sense of humour could be seen when she cracked a joke on how seeing 13-year olds give her nightmares. She effortlessly doesn't take life too seriously.

10. Love Your Body

Lawrence has spoken out numerous times about her body, challenging unrealistic beauty standards. She claimed in an interview with FLARE magazine that she would rather appear overweight on camera (and appear normal) than diet only to dress like a scarecrow. That is a whole lot of body positivity just for you!

Conclusion

Jennifer will teach you profound truths- when she acts, and when she put on a mask that conceals who she truly is. She given up none of her power by leaving the covers on the screen and refusing to act to "fit in" with Hollywood culture.

Chapter 30:

Saying Yes To Things

Today we're going to talk about why saying yes can be a great thing for you and why you should do so especially in social invites.

Life you see is a funny thing. As humans, we tend to see things one dimensionally. And we tend to think that we have a long life ahead of us. We tend to take things for granted. We think we will have time to really have fun and relax after we have retired and so we should spend all our efforts and energy into building a career right now, prioritising it above all else. When faced with a choice between work and play, sometimes many of us, including myself choose work over social invites.

There were periods in my life that i routinely chose work over events that it became such a habit to say no. Especially as an entrepreneur, the interaction between colleagues or being in social events is almost reduced to zero. It became very easy and comfortable to live in this bubble where my one and only priority in life is to work work work. 24 hours, 7 days a week. Of course, in reality a lot of time was wasted on social media and Netflix, but u know, at least i could sort of pretend that i was kind of working all day. And I was sort of being productive and sort of working towards my goals rather than "wasting time on social events". That was what I told myself anyway.

But life does not work that way. As I prioritised work over all else, soon all the social invite offers started drying up. My constant "nos" were becoming evident to my social circle and I was being listed as perpetually unavailable or uninterested in vesting time or energy into any friendships or relationships. And as i retreated deeper and deeper into this black hole of "working remotely" i found myself completely isolated from new experiences and meeting new people, or even completely stopped being involved in any of my friend's lives.

I've successfully written myself out of life and I found myself all alone in it.

Instead of investing time into any meaningful relationships, I found that my closest friends were my laptop, tablet, phone, and television. Technology became my primary way of interacting with the world. And I felt connected, yet empty. I was always plugged in to wifi, but i lived my life through a screen instead of my own two eyes. My work and bedroom became a shell of a home that I spent almost all my time, and life just became sort of pointless. And I just felt very alone.

As I started to feel more and more like something was missing, I couldn't quite make out what it was that led me to this feeling. I simply though to myself, hey I'm prioritising work and my career, making money is what the internet tells me I should do, and not having a life is simply part of the price you have to pay... so why am I so incredibly unhappy?

As it turns out, as I hope many of you have already figured out at this point, that life isn't really just about becoming successful financially. While buying a house, getting a car, and all that good stuff is definitely something that we should strive towards, we should not do so at the expense of our friends. That instead of saying no to them, we should start saying yes, at least once in a while. We need to signal to our friends that hey, yes even though I'm very busy, but I will make an effort to carve out time for you, so that you know I still value you in my life and that you are still a priority.

We need to show our friends that while Monday may not work for us, that I have an opening maybe 2 weeks later if you're still down. That we are still available to grow this friendship.

I came to a point in my life where I knew something had to change. As I started examining my life and the decisions I had made along the way with regards to my career, I knew that what I did wrong was saying no WAAAAAY too often. As I tried to recall when was the last time I actually when I went out with someone other than my one and only BFF, I simply could not. Of the years that went by, I had either said that I was too busy, or even on the off chances that I actually agreed to some sort of meetup, I had the habit of bailing last minute on lunch and dinner appointments with friends. And I never realized that i had such a terrible reputation of being a flaker until I started doing some serious accounting of my life. I had become someone that I absolutely detested without even realising it. I have had people bail on me at the very last minute before, and I hated that feeling. And whenever someone did that to me, I generally found it difficult to ask them out again because I felt that they weren't really that interested in meeting me anyway. That they didn't even bother to reschedule the appointment. And little did I know, I was becoming that very same person and doing the very thing that I hate to my friends. It is no wonder that I started dropping friends like flies with my terrible actions.

As I came to this revelation, I started panicking. It was as if a truck had hit me so hard that I felt that I was in a terrible accident. That how did I let myself get banged up to that extent?

I started scrolling through my contact lists, trying to find friends that might still want to hang out with me. I realized that my WhatsApp was basically dry as a desert, and my calendar was just work for the last 3 years straight with no meaningful highlights, no social events worth noting.

It was at this point that I knew I had made a huge mistake and I needed to change course immediately. Salvaging friendships and prioritising social activities went to the top of my list.

I started creating a list of friends that I had remotely any connection to in the last 5 years and I started asking them out one by one. Some of my friends who i had asked out may not know this, but at that point in my life, i felt pretty desperate and alone and I hung on to every meeting as if my life depended on it. Whilst I did manage to make some appointments and met up with some of them. I soon realized that the damage had been done. That my friends had clearly moved on without me... they had formed their own friends at work and elsewhere, and I was not at all that important to have anymore. It was too little too late at that point and there was not much I could do about it. While I made multiple attempts to ask people out, I did not receive the same offers from people. It felt clearly like a one-way street and I felt that those people that I used to call friends, didn't really see me as one. You see growing a friendship takes time, sometimes years of consistent meetups before this person becomes indispensable in your life. Sharing unique experiences that allow your friends to see that you are truly vested in them and that you care about them and want to spend time with them. I simply did not give myself that chance to be integrated into someone's life in that same way, I did not invest that time to growing those friendships and I paid the price for it.

But I had to learn all these the hard way first before I can receive all the good that was about to come in the future.

In the next piece, I will show how i actually turned my life around by putting myself in positions where I will be exposed to more chances of social activity. And when saying yes became critical to growing a new social network for myself.

Chapter 31:
8 Things To Do When You Like Someone More Than You Thought You Would

Finding someone in life that can be your companion can be quite a journey. You will meet people who like to play games, who are wild and crazy, and those who are just downright unpleasant to be around. You will go on dates that you just want to quickly get out of and head home. But what happens when you meet someone who just seems like the perfect fit for you. When that person seem to sync with you on every wavelength and frequency. What would you do?

You feel your heart bursting out of your chest. You ask yourself is this real life or is it just fantasy (quote from Bohemian Rhapsody if you got that reference)? You felt like you've never connected with someone so deeply and emotionally before and you are just not sure what to make of these intense feelings.

You talk on the phone for hours without running out of things to say. He or she is able to guess your next sentence as if they were reading your mind. And you feel like you've been searching your whole life for this person. Going through guy after guy, or girl after girl, sifting through the noise, and this golden gem has finally presented itself to you.

In today's topic we will go through XX ways that you can do to move forward. Tips on how you can navigate that path forward and make a relationship that lasts a lifetime.

1. Embrace These Feelings

Having butterflies in your stomach or feeling like your heart is overflowing could be signs that you are fully attracted to this person that you've found in your life. They have got your undivided attention and there is no one else that you are thinking of but him or her. Embrace these feelings. Accept that they are there to point a path to you. That you feel these things for a reason. Don't try to brush them aside or hide it under a mat thinking ignorance is bliss. As humans we are feeling creatures, so take these emotions and use them to your advantage.

2. Don't Rush Things

When we like someone a lot, it can be easy for us to get caught up in the moment. We want to see the person every single day and we obsess over their texts and calls. Stop and take a breather. If you want a long-lasting relationship with this person, take things slow. There is no incentive for you to rush things if you foresee a long future ahead. Resist the urge to expect that the person will reciprocate the same intensity at the beginning phases of your relationship. Instead take it one step at a time. Don't rush into bed. Dating takes time.

3. Always Be Yourself

It is easy for us to want to present the best front of ourselves when we are trying to woo the other person that we really like. We may change what we say or do to accommodate the other person because we want them to like us. But if we take it too far, we may lose our sense of identity in the process. Always make sure that you stay true to yourself. The other party has to like you for you, and not who you pretend to be. If that person is right for you, he or she will accept you for who you are and all the quirks that you may bring to the table.

4. Stay Committed To Other Areas of Your Life

Obsessing over someone can become a bad habit for us if we are not mindful of our thoughts and actions. We may have a tendency to prioritise all the time and energy into that person while forgoing all the things we know we should be doing. We lose focus at work, is disinterested in family time, and we may even neglect our friends in the process. Always remember that those are the pillars of your life and to not waver in your commitment to them even though someone new and amazing has entered into your life.

5. Give The Person Time To Warm Up To You

We may feel strongly for the person, but it doesn't necessarily mean that they feel the exact same way about us right away. Building a relationship takes time, and we need to be mindful that things don't simply blossom overnight. A plant takes constant watering and sunlight to flower, and the same goes for courting and dating. Let the person see who you are gradually. Show them a different page of your book to them over time and let them enjoy you from cover to cover rather than giving them a spark-notes summary.

6. Go On Regular Dates

A good way to mesh your two lives together is to go on regular dates. Express little nuggets of interest to them every time you hang out. That way you are releasing some of that built up feelings you have inside you a little at a time. The last thing you want to do is scare the other person away by being too intense and overwhelming. Spending time together is a good way to also see if you are compatible and a good fit for each another.

7. Find New Things To Do Together

Finding new places to hang out, new things to eat, and new things to do, keeps things fresh between the two of you. That way you get to experience what that person is like in different places and settings. You may pick up more on their likes and dislikes that way. Don't forget to take things slow even though you are trying new things together.

8. Take It To The Next Level

If you feel like you've reached a point where you are certain that you like this person, and that he or she feels the same way about you, it may be time to take things to the next level. However long this process takes, ensure that both of you are on the same page. The last thing you want to do is face a rejection or ask too prematurely. Let things happen naturally, that way there is no second guessing.

Conclusion

Managing your feelings for someone you like a lot can be a tricky thing, but hopefully these tips will help you navigate through it all. I sincerely hope that you are able to build a life-long relationship with this treasured person as well. Life is too short to let good people slip by us.

Chapter 32:

<u>6 Ways To Track Your Habits</u>

We are mostly at the front line to judge other people based on their habits and behavior but when it comes to ourselves, there is where we draw the line. We become blind to our habits unless someone else points them out for us. Even if they do, we see their assessment of us as unfair and biased. This is not surprising because such is typical human behavior.

However, how can we assess ad track our habits instead of other people doing it for us? Here are six ways to track your habits:

1. <u>Have A Mentor</u>

A mentor is someone you look up to for leadership, guidance, and inspiration in your life. They are icons of character and success from whom you emulate the positive aspects of their lives. Their importance and the major role they play in shaping our habits is impossible to overlook. You may have mentors for many reasons among them being character development. They contribute immensely in influencing us to develop new habits and as well as track them.

You can track your progress in the adoption of a new habit by gauging yourself with the one who influenced you into it. You can tell whether you are up to standard or out of order regarding your habits. Your mentor becomes the unit of measurement of your progress and you can adjust to fit in.

2. Develop A Routine

A routine is a predictable way of doing things. It is important to have a routine from which you will tell when you stray. Being predictable is not a bad idea entirely. It is a way of checking the boxes of what you have or have not done daily. A routine is important whenever you want to track your habits because it is not biased.

Developing a routine could be difficult but the merits outweigh its demerits. Through a routine, you can perfect desirable habits that you seek to adopt. Practice makes perfect so does the repetition of a habit routinely ingrain it in your personality.

3. Listen To Other People's Opinions About You

What do the people around you say? Have they or have they not observed any notable change in your habits? You would be throwing the baby with the bathwater if you disregard their voices about you. When you hear their opinion, you will know whether you are on or off track regarding the habits you are adopting.

Indeed, people's opinions are not always correct. It could be their perception and not the truth. Regardless, there lies sincerity in unbiased observations by other people on you. They are in a better position to note any change in your habits or routine. You can track your habits through their observations.

4. Benchmark With Your Peers

Your peers are the people with whom you began the journey of adoption of new habits together. Find out whether they are making progress or you are the one lagging. Anything that did not affect their progress and did to yours should concern you. If you have derailed, seek to address what is holding you back.

Through this way, you can hold yourself accountable for your setbacks and forge a way forward. Tracking your habits using your peers' progress challenges your judgment on issues and commitment to resolutions you have made. Do not shy from making a follow-up of your habits through them.

5. Use The Calender

It looks like an analog method of tracking your habits but it has been tried, tested, and proven. Mark important days on your calendar because it creates memories of your journey in changing your habits. It serves as a reminder of a decision you had made which you should pursue to the end.

The most suggested type of calendar is the tangible one because you can see it often unlike the ones in digital form. A calendar will be the silent judge to help you keep track of your habits. Its inaudible judgment will haunt you whenever you see it.

6. Set Milestones

A milestone will consist of a bunch of habits that you seek to adopt. When your eyes are set on a milestone, nothing will distract you away from it. Your focus and energy shall be on completing a milestone.

You can gauge your progress by how many milestones you successfully set and conquered. This will keep you on track when monitoring your habits.

It is advisable to follow these six ways to track your habits if you want to gauge your progress.

Chapter 33:

The Easiest Way to Live a Short, Unimportant Life

An essential and successful life may seem intriguing but, sometimes it's just a lot of work. Whereas, in comparison, a short and unimportant life seems easier to live. The one reason for this may be that you need to eat up your surroundings. People who donate to this world live longer. So, you don't donate. You consume the world. But there is no doubt that people who live longer have many advantages, whereas someone living a short life would not have time for that. Not only is it a loss, but it will affect your life in which you are breathing already.

Few things can lead a person to an unimportant and unhealthy lifestyle. Of course, no one can control how many days we will live on this planet but, we can contribute to our surroundings. And even if you come up with small things, they can impact your life somehow. Be yourself when it comes to shaping. Don't let this world shape you but yourself. It may not only change your life but, it can also give them the confidence to others to change their lives.

It would help if you believed that you could live. If you give up on your life, life will give up on you. Keep yourself worth running in every factor of life. It would be best if you made yourself feel worth it to keep up with the world. Live a meaningful life by all means. How? By contributing to things, talk with a friend, take a long walk in the mornings, or call the people you care about. Even saying hi to a stranger count as contributing to this world. And small contribution leads towards a more significant source of the outcome.

Talk with yourself about how you are going to live this life, and live, not survive. Thet both are different things. We won't know if tomorrow will be our last day, so we got to live it today as it is. Nowadays, we tend to live our lives by ourselves. We prefer to talk on the phone instead of meeting up. It just leads towards an unhealthy and unimportant life. Meet up if you can. Contribute your ideas or decisions to that plan. Make sure that you work out your best if you want it to be done.

A short and unimportant life may seem easier to live by but, it's non-enjoyable. It's full of disadvantages and losses from every side. Isn't it better to live? To give it all your best? We need to devote most of ourselves to this one life that we got. And live each day to its fullest.

Chapter 34:

9 Signs You're Feeling Insecure About a Relationship

Being in a new relationship is often the most exciting part. You go back and forth with your date, wondering if he or she likes you, and you play the dating game as all new romance starts out. But what happens when you start to fall for someone more than you thought you would have liked to at this stage.

It is never a pleasant feeling for us to feel that we are not in control, but that is the process of being vulnerable and admitting to yourself that you do have a personal investment in this relationship. If you are unsure about what you are going through,

Here are 7 Signs That Show You Are Feeling Insecure About A Relationship:

1.   You Start Checking Their "Last Seen"

We have all done this before - We wonder why it takes so long for the person to reply our texts so we check our messaging apps constantly to check when they were last online. We then draw deductions that they may have deliberately chosen not to reply to our messages despite being online. However unhealthy habit of checking their "last seen" only takes power away from our self-worth. We need to stop obsessing over such small little details and just focus on the things we are supposed to do for the day. If the person genuinely likes you, he or she will find the time to reply in a thoughtful and appropriate manner.

2.   You Anxiously Hope That They Ask You Out

Waiting for the next date to happen is normal. We all expect to have some back and forth to ensure that it is not a one-sided effort in dating and relationships. However, if this becomes an anxious wait, then you might be falling into the realm of insecurity. Ideally things should happen naturally if all is going well. If you catch yourself losing sleep because he or she hasn't asked you out, take some of that power back and consider taking the initiative instead to either ask if there is going to be a next date, or even asking them out if you want to see this through. Don't let anxiety rule your dating life.

3.   You Wait For Them To Say Something Sweet To Affirm Their Like of you

We all want to be woo-ed. It is a nice feeling when someone says something sweet to you just because. But if you find yourself eagerly anticipating every sentence to be something affectionate, be careful not to be disappointed if it doesn't happen ever-so-often. Dating and relationships can be a tricky business; we don't want to seem too needy or too forward at the same time. Sometimes we just have to find a balance between being overly sweet and also reserving some of it when so as not to come across too strong.

4. You Start Thinking Of The Worst-Case Scenarios

Being in the early phases of a relationship is always fun, but as the dust settles and you start thinking of the worst-case scenarios, you may be feeling insecure. We all want to go back to the part of dating where we expect nothing from the other party - we are dating a few different people at once and we have no desires to commit. But when you start catching yourself thinking of what could go wrong with someone you've decided you like more than others, it may be time to take a step back and reassess the situation. Don't jump too far ahead of the curve.

5. You Can't Focus On Your Work

Being in love and thinking about the wonderful things about the other person is a normal way to lose focus on your work. However if this lack of concentration starts revolving around worry that things could go wrong, or that the person may not like you, then you've got to snap out of it. It is never healthy to let these negative thoughts affect your daily productivity. Remember that your life always comes first - Focus on the important things and then worry about dating and relationships later.

6. You're Distraught From The Lack of Clear Signals

You find yourself second guessing everything. One minute you think your date is interested, the next you're worried he or she is not. This back and forth can take a toll on your mental capacity to handle things and you may find yourself feeling out of sorts. You wonder if your date went well or did it go disastrously. The fact that your date isn't giving you any clear signs adds to your insecurity about the whole thing.

7. You're Unsure About Where This Is Going

Similar to the previous point, this time you are unsure where this relationship is headed. Is there something there or should you cut your losses and move on. It will be hard to assess the situation and the only way to be sure is to ask him or her directly what their thoughts are about the whole matter. If they are unable to give you a clear answer, you can at least be assured that it is not all in your head. Do what is best for yourself and never be too hung up over just one person.

8. You Wonder If They Are Seeing Someone Else

This is insecurity at one of the highest levels. Trust is something that must be built over time. If you find yourself questioning whether your date or partner is seeing someone else, maybe you never really felt secure in this relationship in the first place. This could be a tricky matter to handle so once again if you find yourself doubting every aspect of this bond, maybe it's time to be dial it back until you can trust your whole heart with that person.

9. You Question Every Single Decision You Make

Second guessing ourselves and everything that we do has got to be one of the worst ways to operate in life. You question whether you said the right thing on the date, whether you made the right moves, whether you came off as confident rather weak. These are questions that we need to not bother ourselves with because it will not bring any goodness to us. Make decisions that you will stick with no matter what and stop ruminating on the past. Just do what you can now and move forward with pride.

Conclusion

Dating and relationships are not easy. It comes with its own set of rules and emotions are bound to run rampant at some point if we don't reign them in. Instead of making it harder than it already is for ourselves, simply trust that things will work out if it's meant to be. Overthinking and feeling insecure will not bring us any good. The fact is that sometimes we will get our hearts broken, but we will stand tall and learn from our past. The quest for love is not going to be a piece of cake, but if the right person comes along, things will work out.

CPSIA information can be obtained
at www.ICGtesting.com
Printed in the USA
LVHW081956130122
708314LV00013B/487